ACCELERATED

PIANO *Adventures*® *by Nancy and Randall Faber*

T0086932

CONTENTS

About the "Sightreading Stocking Stuffers"

A student's enthusiasm for learning Christmas music can become an opportunity to create enthusiasm for sightreading. In this book, each Christmas song is presented with short melodies, called "Sightreading Stocking Stuffers."

The "Sightreading Stocking Stuffers" are **melodic variations** of the carol being studied. Teachers will notice that the lyrics and rhythm patterns are from the carol. By drawing on these familiar rhythms, the student may effectively focus on interval reading and note reading.

The student should sightread one "stocking stuffer" a day while learning the Christmas song. Or, the stocking stuffers can be used as sightreading during the lesson itself.

The teacher may wish to tell the student:

> **Sightreading means "reading music at first sight."**
>
> When sightreading, music is not practiced over and over. Instead, it is only played several times with the highest concentration.

The following **3 C's** may help the student with sightreading:

 CORRECT HAND POSITION
Find the correct starting note for each hand.

 COUNT - OFF
Set a steady tempo by counting one "free" measure
before starting to play.

 CONCENTRATE
Focus your eyes on the music, carefully reading the intervals.

FF1209

Stuffing the Stockings

Each musical "gift" is an interval: **2nd**, **3rd**, **4th**, or **5th**.
Draw a line connecting each "gift" to the correct stocking.

Extra Credit: Play each "gift" on the piano using the fingering given.

Good King Wenceslas

Moderately

Traditional

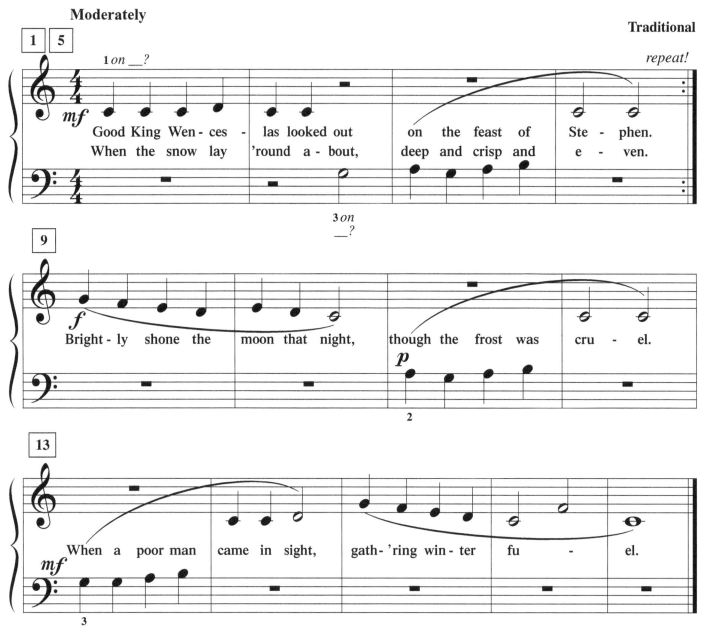

1 **5**

1 on __?

repeat!

mf

Good King Wen - ces - las looked out | on the feast of | Ste - phen.
When the snow lay 'round a - bout, | deep and crisp and | e - ven.

9

3 on __?

f

Bright - ly shone the | moon that night, | though the frost was | cru - el.

p

13

mf

When a poor man | came in sight, | gath- 'ring win - ter | fu - el.

Teacher Duet: (Student plays *1 octave higher*)

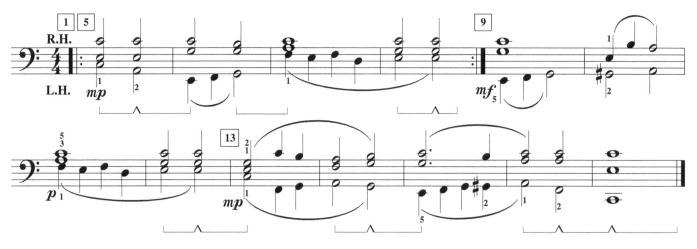

FF1209

Sightread one "stocking stuffer" a day
while you are learning the carol.
The words to the "stocking stuffers" are
familiar, but the **melodies have changed**!

Circle the stocking after sightreading.

("variations" for sightreading)

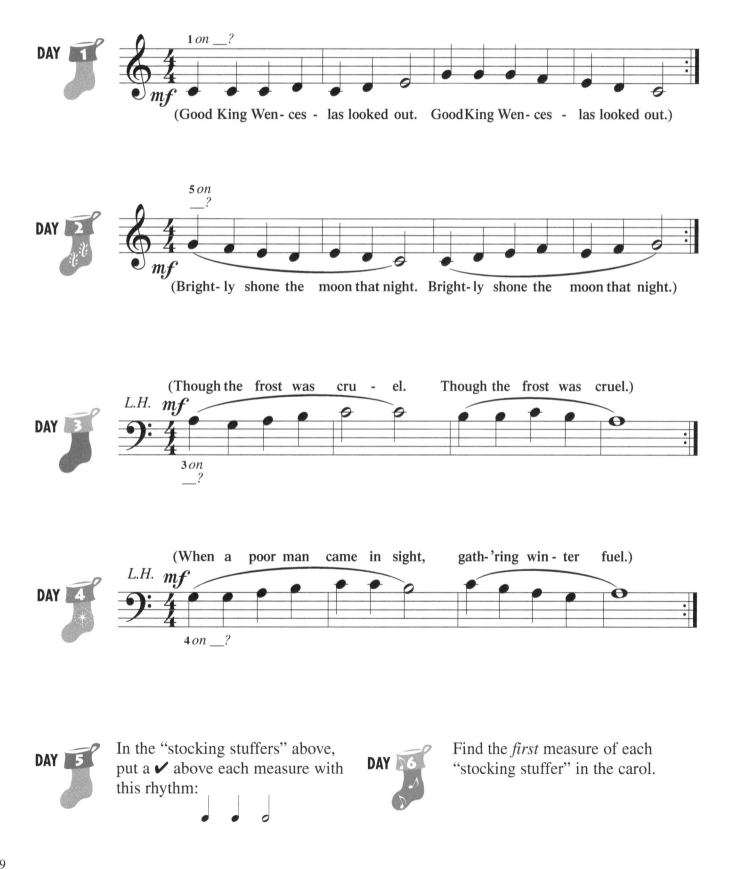

Angels We Have Heard on High

Quickly, with joy

Traditional

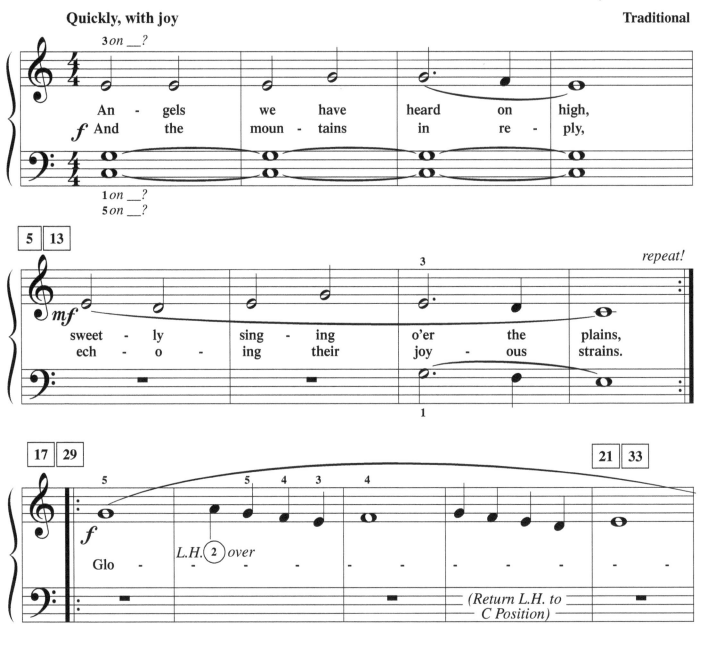

Teacher Duet: (Student plays *1 octave higher*)

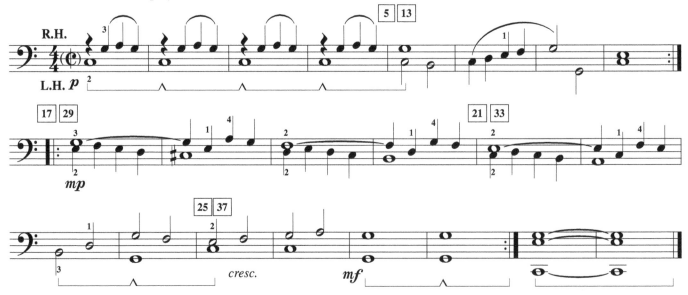

FF1209

- - - - - ri - a

{ in   ex -
  in   ex -

①

Repeat from measure 17.

cel - sis   De - o!
cel - sis   De - o!

Sightread one "stocking stuffer" a day
while learning *Angels We Have Heard on High*.

Circle the stocking after sightreading.

CHRISTMAS STOCKING STUFFERS

("variations" for sightreading)

DAY 1

1 *on* __?

f (An - gels   we   have   heard   on   high,)

DAY 2

(Sweet - ly   sing - ing   o'er   the   plains.)

mf 3 *on* __?

DAY 3

5 *on* __?

mf (Glo - - - - - - ri - a.)

DAY 4 Can you find the melody of **Day 2** in the carol? Hint: It is in the treble clef.

DAY 5 Can you sing from *measure 17* to the end of the carol?

Silent Night

Words by Joseph Mohr
Music by Franz Grüber

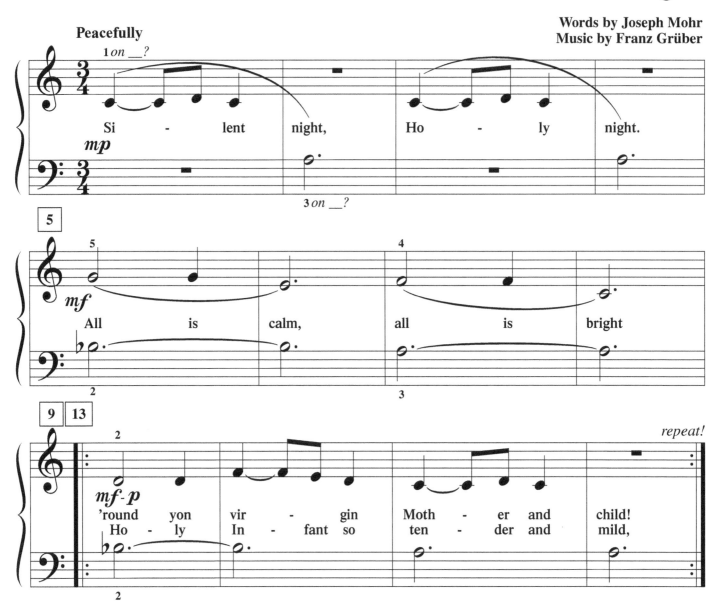

Si - lent night, Ho - ly night.

All is calm, all is bright

'round yon vir - gin Moth - er and child!
Ho - ly In - fant so ten - der and mild,

Teacher Duet: (Student plays *1 octave higher*)

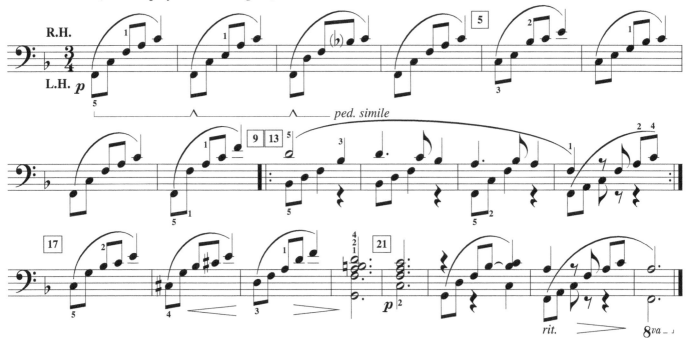

FF1209

17

5 *change to* ③ 5 3 1 2

Sleep in heav - en - ly peace.

3

21

2

Sleep in heav - en - ly peace!

p

1 2 4

Sightread one "stocking stuffer" a day
while learning *Silent Night.*

Circle the stocking after sightreading!

PEACEFUL STOCKING STUFFERS

("variations" for sightreading)

DAY 1

2 on
___?

(Si - lent night.)

mp

2 on ___?

DAY 2

5 on ___?

mf (All is calm,)

2 on ___?

DAY 3

4 on ___?

mf (All is bright.)

3 on ___?

DAY 4

1 on ___?

p (Moth - er and child.)

1 on ___?
3 on ___?

DAY 5 In *Silent Night,* circle each
measure with this rhythm:

DAY 6 Which other "stocking stuffer" has
the same rhythm used for **Day 1**?

Day ____

Teacher Note: The student may play the
♩. ♪ rhythm by imitation or rote.

Joy to the World

Words by Isaac Watts
Music by G. F. Handel

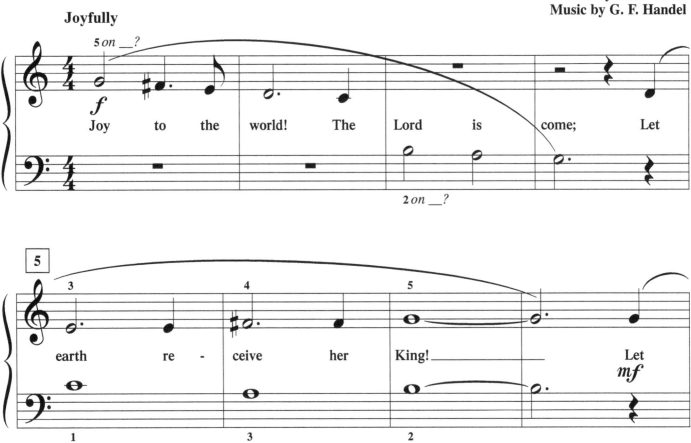

Joyfully

Joy to the world! The Lord is come; Let

earth re - ceive her King! _____ Let

Teacher Duet: (Student plays *1 octave higher*)

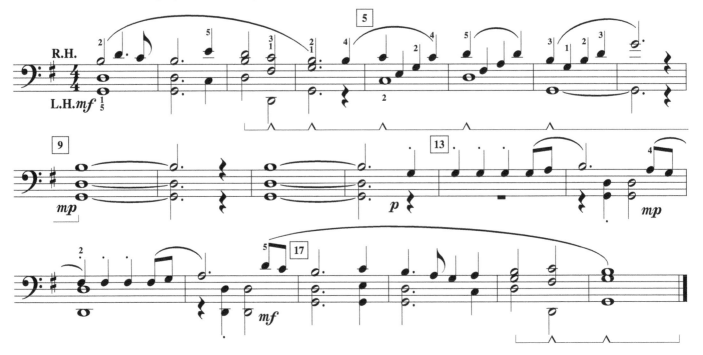

FF1209

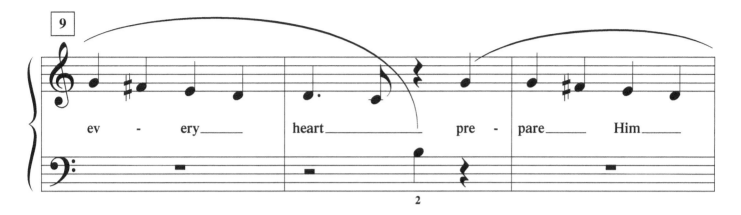

ev - ery___ heart___ pre - pare___ Him___

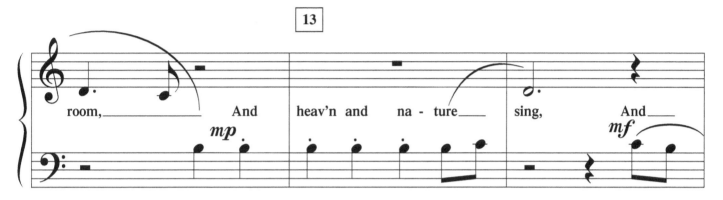

room,___ And heav'n and na - ture___ sing, And___

mp *mf*

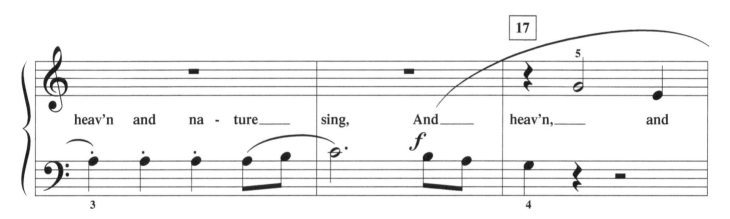

heav'n and na - ture___ sing, And___ heav'n,___ and

f

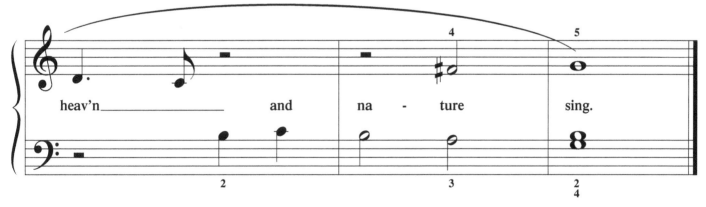

heav'n___ and na - ture sing.

(The Stocking Stuffers for *Joy to the World* are on page 12.)

Sightread one "stocking stuffer" a day while learning *Joy to the World.*

Circle the stocking after sightreading.

("variations" for sightreading)

The pairs of eighth notes (♫) in the carol always fall on:

beat 1   **beat 2**   **beat 3**   **beat 4**

(circle one)

Put a ✔ above the phrase in the carol that has a **tie** and a **slur**.

Jingle Bells

Words and Music by
J. Pierpont

Lively

Dash - ing through the snow in a one-horse o - pen sleigh;

O'er the fields we go, laugh - ing all the way.

Bells on bob - tail ring, mak - ing spir - its bright; What

fun it is to ride and sing a sleigh - ing song to - night! Oh!

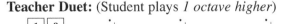

Teacher Duet: (Student plays *1 octave higher*)

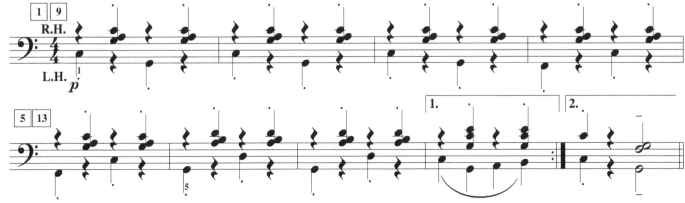

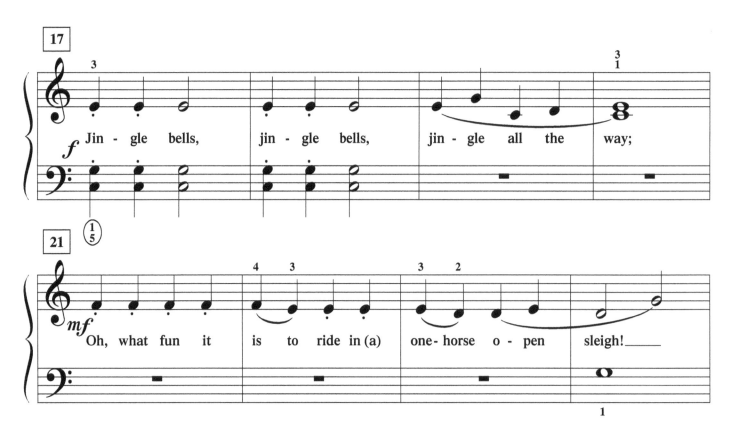

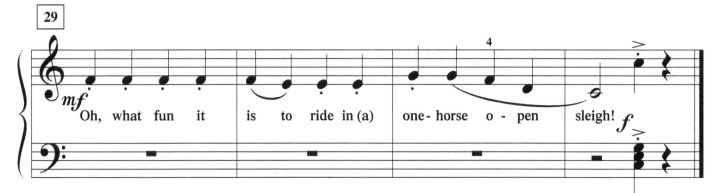

14

Sightread one "stocking stuffer" a day
while learning *Jingle Bells*.

Circle the stocking after sightreading!

SLEIGHBELL STOCKING STUFFERS

("variations" for sightreading)

DAY 1

3 *on*
___?

mp
Jin - gle   all the,   *p*   jin - gle, jin - gle,   jin - gle all the   way.

1 *on* ___?
5 *on* ___?

DAY 2

mf
Oh, what fun it   is   to ride in (a) one - horse o - pen   sleigh!

5 *on*
___?

DAY 3

5 *on*
___?

mf
One - horse   o - pen,   one - horse o - pen   sleigh.

1
3
5

DAY 4

5 *on* ___?
1 *on* ___?

p
Jin - gle bells,   jin - gle bells,   jin - gle all the   way.

f.   *f.*

1 *on* ___?
5 *on* ___?

Can you sing page 14 of *Jingle Bells* without playing the piano?

DAY 5

F1209

We Three Kings of Orient Are

Words and Music by
J. H. Hopkins, Jr.

Flowing smoothly

mf We three kings of O - ri - ent are
bear - ing gifts, we trav - erse a - far.

Field and foun - tain, moor and moun - tain, fol - low - ing

yon - der star. Oh,_____ Star of won - der,
Star of roy - al

Teacher Duet: (Student plays *1 octave higher*)

FF1209

Repeat from measure 18.

26

star   of   night!
beau   -   ty   bright!

West   -   ward   lead   -   ing,   still   pro   -

mf

move (1) *to A*

30

ceed   -   ing,   guide   us   to   Thy   per   -   fect   light.

move (1) *to A*

Sightread one "stocking stuffer" a day while learning *We Three Kings of Orient Are.*

Circle the stocking after sightreading.

⭐ **S** **TARRY STOCKING STUFFERS**

("variations" for sightreading)

DAY 1
3 *on* ___?
mf
(We   three   kings   of   O - ri - ent   are.)

DAY 2
mf (Field   and   foun - tain,   moor   and   moun - tain.)
1 *on* ___?

DAY 3
mf (Star   of   roy - al   beau - ty   bright!)
1 *on* ___?
3 *on* ___?
5 *on* ___?

DAY 4   Write the counts "1 - 2 - 3" under the beats for **Day 3**.

DAY 5   Circle the most common rhythm in *We Three Kings of Orient Are.*

♩ ♩ ♩   or   ♩ ♩   or   ♩.

FF1209

17

Deck the Halls

Merrily

Traditional

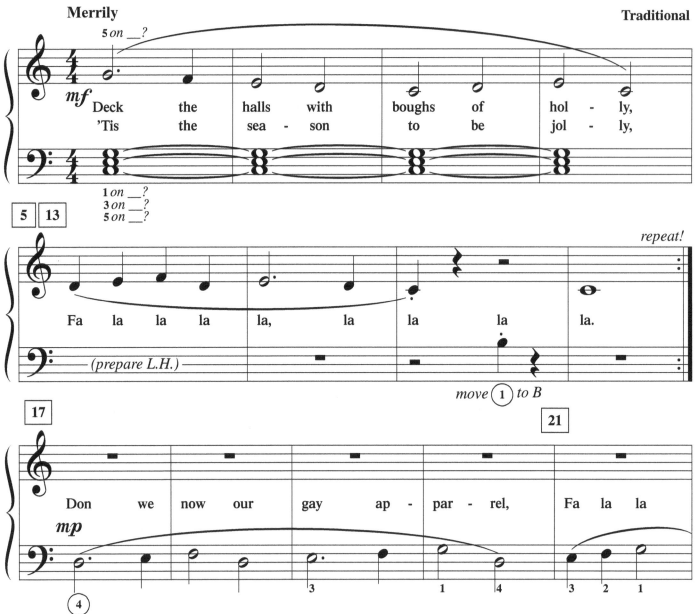

Deck the halls with boughs of hol - ly,
'Tis the sea - son to be jol - ly,

Fa la la la la, la la la la.

(prepare L.H.)

repeat!

move ① to B

Don we now our gay ap - par - rel, Fa la la

Teacher Duet: (Student plays *1 octave higher*)

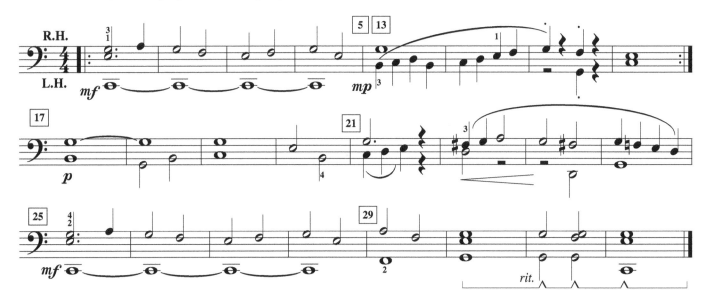

Sightread one "stocking stuffer" a day while learning *Deck the Halls.*

Circle the stocking after sightreading.

FA LA LA STOCKING STUFFERS

("variations" for sightreading)

DAY 1

1 *on*
___?

mf

(Deck   the   halls   with   boughs   of   hol - ly.)

DAY 2

mf (Fa   la   la   la   la   la   la   la   la.)

1 *on*
___?

DAY 3

2 *on*
___?

mf (Fa   la   la   la   la,   la   la   la   la.)

DAY 4 — Circle all the **5ths** in the "stocking stuffers" above.

DAY 5 — Circle the rhythm each time it appears in *Deck the Halls.*

Hint: It occurs 6 times.

Teacher Note: Some students may wish to substitute the ♩. ♪ rhythm in measures 7, 12, and 19.

O Come, All Ye Faithful
(Adeste Fideles)

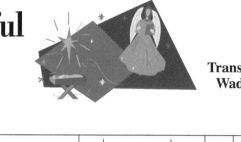

Transcribed by F. Oakeley
Wade's *"Cantus Diversi"*

Moderately

O come, all ye faith - ful, joy - ful and tri - um - phant, O

come ye, O come____ ye to Beth - le - hem. *lift!*

Come and be - hold Him, born the King of an - gels. O *softly!*

(prepare L.H.)

Teacher Duet: (Student plays *1 octave higher*)

R.H.

L.H. *mf*

p

mp

cresc.

mf

FF1209

Sightread one "stocking stuffer" a day while learning *O Come, All Ye Faithful.*

Circle the stocking after sightreading.

JOYFUL STOCKING STUFFERS

("variations" for sightreading)

DAY 1

3 on ___?

mf

(Joy - ful and tri - um - phant, joy - ful and tri - um - phant.)

DAY 2

(O come ye, O come__ ye to Beth - le - hem.)

mf

1 on ___?

DAY 3

(O come let us a - dore Him;__ Christ,__ the Lord.)

f

3 on ___?

DAY 4 Circle a C chord in the carol.

DAY 5 Circle and label a **2nd**, a **3rd**, a **4th**, and a **5th** in the "stocking stuffers" above.

The *secondo* is the lower part in a 4-hand piano duet.

Duet Hints:

- Notice the pick-up note on **beat 3**.
  Prepare your hand position and *listen*
  for the primo player to count off, "1-2-3, 1-2."

- Observe all the dynamic marks.

- Lift your hands with your partner's
  hands at the end of the duet.

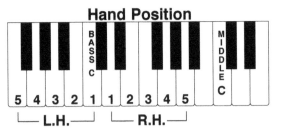

We Wish You
a Merry Christmas

Secondo (student part)

The *primo* is the top part in a 4-hand piano duet.

Duet Hints:

- Notice the pick-up note on **beat 3**. Prepare your hand position, then set a steady beat by counting aloud, "1-2-3, 1-2."

- Observe all the dynamic marks.

- Lift your hands with your partner's hands at the end of the duet.

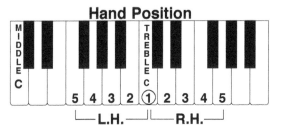

We Wish You a Merry Christmas

Primo (student part)

Christmas Music Calendar

Complete the music calendar for each day of December.